VISION THAT WORKS:
TURNING YOUR CHURCH'S
VISION INTO ACTION

It's been great having you part of prayer group

Blessings

Dave

VISION THAT WORKS

Turning Your Church's Vision into Action

Dave Collins

Vision That Works: Turning your Church's Vision into Action

Copyright ©2008 David Collins
All rights reserved
Printed in Canada
International Standard Book Number: 978-1-894860-38-3

Co-published by:
Castle Quay Books
1-1295 Wharf Street, Pickering, Ontario, L1W 1A2
Tel: (416) 573-3249   Fax: (416) 981-7922
E-mail: info@castlequaybooks.com
www.castlequaybooks.com

Tyndale Academic Press
25 Ballyconnor Court, Toronto, Ontario, M2M 4B3
lwillard@tyndale.ca
416-226-6620 x2657

Copy editing by Marina H. Hofman
Cover design by Essence Publishing
Printed at Essence Publishing, Belleville, Ontario

Library and Archives Canada Cataloguing in Publication
Collins, David, 1949-
     Vision that works: turning your church's vision into action / David
Collins. -- Rev. ed.
Includes bibliographical references.
ISBN 978-1-894860-38-3

     1. Church growth. 2. Church renewal. 3. Pastoral theology. I.
Title.
BV652.25.C614 2008   254   C2008-900738-7

To: My wife, Linda, for her unfailing love.
My children, Matt and Rachel, for their constant
encouragement.
The guys in my small group for believing in me.
The folks of Carruthers Creek for allowing me to fail.
Eric for introducing me to the planning process.

CONTENTS

INTRODUCTION

Pastor John sat in the back of the auditorium and watched as the worship team rehearsed for Sunday's service. It had been a while since he had sat in the back row of any church, let alone at Woodridge. Things definitely looked different from back there. He almost felt detached from what was going on at the front. "I wonder if that's how the people who sit back here week after week feel, 'detached.'"

It made sense in a strange sort of way. If the platform was the heart of church life, the farther you were from it, the more removed you were from what was going on, and the more removed you were, the less likely you were to be committed to what the church was doing. "Maybe that's the problem," he mused, "too many people in the back row."

As he sat looking over the empty pews, another thought crossed his mind. If this analogy was in any way representative of the challenge his church was facing, then the solution was simply a matter of getting people to move closer to the front—

getting them involved in the action.

"Yeah, right," he thought, remembering the chilly reception he had received the Sunday he invited those in the back row to move closer to the front. "You'd have thought I'd asked them to sacrifice their first-born."

"No," he concluded, "it isn't going to be that easy, but somehow I have to connect with the people in the back row, those who don't seem to be involved."

Woodridge Community Church wasn't always stuck in a rut. There was a time when you could feel the excitement in the air. God was active in the life of the church and the people. The church had been planted by a church in the city core. Those who were part of the original group had been totally committed to the project. They thought nothing of spending two or three nights a week serving in some capacity. When something needed to be done, they were willing to roll up their sleeves and do it, even if it meant sacrifice—after all, this was God's work. Then the building project began. It seemed like everybody got involved. The work crews, the cleanup, it didn't matter what the task, there was always someone willing to give a hand.

But when the building was finished, it seemed that the people let out one huge collective breath and sat in the back row.

It didn't happen all at once. In the early days, when they first moved in, there was still a lot to do and the church was still growing. In a few short months, their numbers had almost doubled. In fact, the original people felt a little out of place. "It's not that we don't want the new people to come," one man remarked.

"It's just that it doesn't seem like our church anymore." And there it was, that ever so subtle shift. When once the people spoke of "our vision" to reach the community, they now began to talk about "our church" with an almost possessive attitude.

That was almost three years ago. Since then, it seemed that they had settled into a groove. Once in a while someone new would show up, a few even stayed and got involved, but somewhere along the way the congregation had lost its reason for existing, and John didn't know how to get it back.

•••••••••••••

Pastor John is not alone in his frustration. A study conducted by the Barna Research Group demonstrated that "of the approximately 350,000 churches in America, four out of five are either plateaued or shrinking."[1] Tom Rainer in his research observes, "Only one person is reached for Christ every year for every eighty-five church members in America."[2]

Is this a crisis of faith? Are people giving up on Christianity? If I understand the research of Reginald Bibby, noted Canadian sociologist, the answer is a resounding "No."[3] In fact, just the opposite is true. Christianity is alive and well, just not in the church, at least not the traditional church.

So where does this leave pastors who are struggling not to just plug the leaks but to actually move their churches to a place where they are healthy, growing, Christ-centred communities?

I want to say at the outset that there are no quick fixes when it comes to growing a church. The principles I share in this book come from my own experience as a pastor, who for 21 years struggled with these very issues and who by the grace of God was blessed with the privilege of serving a very loving and accepting congregation. Along the way, through trial and error, many mistakes and the counsel of some very wise men, God taught me some things about leading a congregation, about mission, vision and values, and particularly about the process of planning that I believe can help churches get out of that quagmire of mediocrity and on the road to health.

This book is not intended to be a cure-all or a one-size-fits-all solution but rather to provide you with some tools. Consequently, what is shared will likely need to be adapted to your individual context. To this end you will find some templates in the appendix to help you in the planning process. You are free to use them in any way you like.

One more comment: if my experience is any measure of reality when it comes to planning, churches can easily dismiss the idea on the grounds it is unspiritual or that it is only for larger churches. I couldn't disagree more. The call of Christ to count the cost of following Him implies an element of planning, particularly in the illustrations He gives of building a tower or going to war. Planning doesn't rule out the work of the Spirit in any sense; it merely helps us decide from among a number of things we could do which ones we believe will be most effective for the kingdom in our circumstance, by God's grace.

As for working in large churches, let me respond with an expression one of the men on my board used to say to me: "To fail to plan is to plan to fail, and it doesn't matter how big you are."

It is also worth noting that while this process can be worked through internally, it is often more effective, particularly the first time around, with the help of an outside facilitator. He or she can say things the pastor or others in leadership are often not able to say. Don't be afraid to employ a consultant; it is money well spent.

Time to Ask Why

"Many are the plans in a man's heart, but it is the LORD's
purpose that prevails."

Prov. 19:21

"Our church," John thought, "...interesting how one little
phrase can say so much." People who had been part of the core
group were saying, "It doesn't feel like 'our' church anymore." At
the time, they were reacting to all the new folks of course, but
after a while the "our church" no longer referred to the invasion
of new people; instead it became the unspoken value that
seemed to dominate all of the activities of Woodridge
Community Church.

"Where did we ever get the idea that this thing we call church
is 'ours,' that it somehow belongs to 'us?'" wondered John. "No
one would actually say that of course; if asked, we would tell you
we are about winning the lost and bringing them into the church.
In truth, however, we like things just the way they are."

"Maybe," John thought, "that's why my attempts to reach out to the community always seem to meet with such resistance. In reality we don't want to grow, we don't want new people to come to the church. We are comfortable serving ourselves."

As John reflected on these things he found himself wondering if it was time to revisit why the church even existed.

●●●●●●●●●●●●●●●

WHY DOES THE CHURCH EXIST?

It's a question I believe every pastor, every church board or leadership team, and every church member should ask on a regular basis. I say this because I don't believe for a moment there is a church in North America, or anywhere for that matter, that sets out to be self-serving. No one starts a church with the idea that it will only meet the needs of those who are part of the planting group. Just the opposite; church planting is always undertaken with a view to winning the lost and bringing them into the body of Christ. This being the case, how is it that churches go off the rails so quickly, generally within one generation?

I believe the answer is tied directly to how we respond to the question, "Why does the church exist?"

You see, when a church is young, when it is in its infancy, the people who make up the church are close to the action. They have a clear sense of calling. When they say "our church," they really do mean God's church and they really do want to accomplish His purposes. As time goes on, however, something happens to those who started the church. You might say that they get moved to the back row to make room for the newcomers. When this happens, the founding congregants can easily become disconnected. The *our* in "our church" becomes more about what they want, what makes them comfortable, than what God might want.

At the same time, those who join apart from new believers, tend to also move into the back row. These folks often come from other churches and bring with them a mixed bag of ideas about why the church exists, most of which have to do with meeting their needs. As a result, they seldom hold the same passion for the ministry or the same desire to be involved in reaching the lost. Failure to focus on why the church exists or to teach about the mission of the church only enhances this self-serving mindset.

> As a result, they seldom hold the same passion for the ministry or the same desire to be involved in reaching the lost. Failure to focus on why the church exists or to teach about the mission of the church only enhances this self-serving mindset.

It's also a question to which there are two potential answers. The one is a reflection of how we are in reality functioning and the other a reflection of what Jesus intended His church to be doing.

Rick Warren, in his book *The Purpose Driven Church*, does an excellent job of identifying the biblical mandate that God gives the church and appropriately points out, "It isn't our job to create the purposes of the church but to discover them."[4]

It would seem to me then, if we are all using the same Bible to discover these purposes, we should all in fact have basically the same purpose or mission and therefore the same mission statement.

It also follows that as long as the Bible remains unchanged, the purposes of the church will also remain unchanged.

Simply put, the mission of the church is what God tells us, in the Bible, we should be doing. This mission doesn't change from one church to another, nor does it change from one generation to another.

This is important to realize, because in my own journey and in many of the churches I have been asked to consult with, there is a lot of confusion around the idea of mission and what exactly a mission statement should be. This is especially true when the concept of vision is introduced into the mix.

So, for the sake of clarity and for the purpose of this book, I am going to define "mission" simply as "what we do as a church."

At Carruthers Creek Community Church, where I pastored for 21 years, we came up with the following mission statement, after a number of rather wordy efforts:

"The mission of Carruthers Creek Community Church is to enable people of all ages to become fully devoted followers of Jesus Christ."

This is in fact a condensed contemporary statement of the "Great Commission" of Matthew 28:19-20.

Any mission statement that fails to include some form of the Great Commission has missed the point of church. I believe

one can convinc-
ingly argue that to
make disciples
covers every mean-
ingful activity of

> **Any mission statement that fails to include some form of the Great Commission has missed the point of church.**

the church. To make a disciple, one first must evangelize—
whether locally or overseas. It further implies that when someone is a disciple he ia growing in his own spiritual understanding of God, and that comes at least in part through the teaching
ministries of the church. Being disciples means being like Christ
in the way we care for and minister to one another, both in and
outside the church. And being a disciple of Christ means being
a worshiper of God.

Apart from these kinds of ministries, in 21 years of pastoral
ministry I haven't been able to think of anything else that we
should be doing as the body of Christ.

So what's the problem?

Exactly what Pastor John concluded: we don't visit our mission often enough. I don't mean we need to preach from
Matthew 28 more often, although for some it might not be a
bad idea to include it at least once a year. Rather, we need to
teach the relationship or connection between the topic or pas-
sage of the day and what it means to be a disciple of Christ. This
has to happen on a regular basis; after all, this is our mission.

A word of warning: should you choose to remind people of
the mission of the church in this manner and with any frequen-
cy, you will come under criticism. Do not let this discourage

you. Stay the course; better to be criticized—and I say this from experience—for preaching too often on this topic of disciple making than not enough. Sooner or later people will catch on and get involved in the mission.

A MISSION STATEMENT FOR YOUR CHURCH

The question might well be asked, "If all churches have the same purpose or mission, what's the point of a mission statement?"

The value of a mission statement for your church lies not in its uniqueness but in its function. It serves as a rallying cry for the troops. That's why I believe it should be short and to the point. At Carruthers Creek we would often use an abbreviated statement that simply read "Making fully devoted followers."

> The value of a mission statement for your church lies not in its uniqueness but in its function. It serves as a rallying cry for the troops.

I appreciate that this may differ a little from what a number of the books on this topic say. Rick Warren talks about a "Purpose Statement" and includes in it a rather lengthy list of what the church does to make disciples. In doing so, by his own admission, he tends to combine or tie together the ideas of purpose and vision. I'm not suggesting this is wrong. However, if we accept Aubrey Malphurs' definition of vision as "a clear and challenging picture of the future of a ministry as identified by leadership," then this approach runs into difficulty.[5] Making disciples is what we do; it's not a picture of the future. How we go about making disciples in a given time and cultural context—that's a vision of the future.

So, "mission" and therefore a "mission statement" is what we do as the church of Jesus Christ, and we do it no matter where in the world we are, until Christ returns.

The value of this approach lies first in its simplicity. It allows us to state in a very concise way what we are about, even to the point of creating a memorable phrase that captures the imagination of the congregation. More importantly, it provides us with an evaluation tool by inviting leadership to ask the question of any ministry undertaken by the church. "Does this contribute to the making of a disciple?" If we cannot easily see the connection, then maybe it is something we shouldn't be doing.

> So, "mission" and therefore a "mission statement" is what we do as the church of Jesus Christ, and we do it no matter where in the world we are, until Christ returns.

Aubrey Malphurs, in one of his latest books, *Advanced Strategic Planning*, points out that a mission statement should help you personalize the Great Commission for your particular church.[6] In this way people can more readily identify with it. Thus, including the name of your church in the mission statement adds strength to it.

●●●●●●●●●●●●●●

John had no idea when he embarked on this journey how difficult it would be. He could still see the looks on the faces of the board members when he first presented the idea of drafting a mission statement.

"Why would we do that?" responded Paul, the board chairman. "We already know what we are supposed to be doing. The Bible is clear; we are here to worship God!"

"Now wait just a moment," said Anne. "I'm not so sure there isn't more to it than that; what about prayer and caring for one another?"

"And don't forget teaching the Bible," added Ralph.

It was clear John had his work cut out for him and it took several meetings before they finally settled on a statement that everyone could agree on.

"The mission of Woodridge Community Church is to make devoted followers of Christ from all those who live in our community and the world."

Next John proposed that the statement be presented to the congregation through a series of Sunday morning messages. He also suggested that the board be available after each service to answer any questions the congregation might have concerning the mission statement.

They were all for the series but had some reservations about the question-and-answer process. "You're the one who is best equipped to answer questions, Pastor, we don't need to be up there."

"No," John insisted, "it is important that the congregation see that this is not just something I dreamed up but, as the leadership, together we believe this is what God is calling us to do."

The series went well, and people seemed to get excited about the mission. The board stood together at the front after the service and fielded questions from the congregation. As they did, John sensed a noticeable change in their confidence. They really were uniting around the mission. He was sure he'd hit the jackpot. "Now the church would start to come alive," he thought, "the way it was in those earlier years."

2

DOES ANYONE KNOW WHERE WE'RE GOING?

"The LORD said to Abram, 'Leave your country, your
people and your father's household and go to the land I
will show you. I will make you into a great nation and I
will bless you.'"

Gen. 12:1-2

John found himself sitting in the back row of the auditorium again, only this time he was alone. No music rehearsal to distract him. He had come here to think, to get perspective.

Following the presentation of the mission statement people seemed to be excited. He really thought he had landed on the solution to the church's slump. Mary, one of the elders, had even taken the initiative to get an abbreviated form of the statement embroidered on some golf shirts and gave one to each member of the leadership team. Others in the church asked if they could buy one. It really felt like new life had been breathed into the church.

That was six months ago and a lot had happened since then. Glen, one of the key leaders, got transferred to another city. The Smiths, one of the founding families, left the church claiming the mission focused too much on evangelism and not enough on needs of the existing congregation. The congregation as a whole, while they liked the idea of the mission statement, didn't seem to get it—at least not if their actions were any indication. It appeared as though nothing had changed. They just kept doing church the way they always had.

John tried not to let it get to him, but he had to admit, some days it was downright discouraging. "What is missing?" he wondered, as he sat alone in the sunlit sanctuary. "How is it they were able to stay so focused during the planting process and then again during the building process, only to lose that focus not long after these phases were complete?"

As he sat reflecting on these things his mind went back to the building years. Even to this day a chill would run down his spine when he remembered the morning they showed the congregation the model of the new building. The applause that broke out spontaneously and the excitement—it was as if in that moment the congregation caught a glimpse of what the future was going to look like, a glimpse that seemed to infuse them with energy.

That's when it hit John. "We need a glimpse of what the future might look like if we are going to be faithful to the mission. We need a vision!"

●●●●●●●●●●●●●●

In his quest to breathe new life into Woodridge Community Church, John had stumbled onto something and at the same time stumbled over it.

He had stumbled onto the idea that the people needed to be reminded of why they did church and that God really did have a mission for them. Furthermore, stating the mission clearly and concisely gave the congregation a sense of purpose.

At the same time John had stumbled over this same truth when he assumed that framing a mission statement and teaching it would be enough to sustain energy and commitment.

Unfortunately this is a mistake churches and many secular organizations often make. They formulate a mission statement, paste it all over their literature and then wonder why it doesn't elicit commitment.

Long-term commitment requires more than just knowing what to do. It requires a reason to keep doing what we do, and further it requires that we show people what happens when we do what we do. In other words, we have to show them the model.

Aubrey Malphurs defines vision as "a clear and challenging picture of the future of the ministry as you believe it can and must be."[7]

> Long-term commitment requires more than just knowing what to do.

Implicit in painting a picture of the future is detail. When an architect prepares a model of a subdivision or a large complex, the buildings are often represented by blocks. These blocks may be shaped in the rough form of the structures to be built on that site, but there is little detail to show what the buildings will look like when they are complete.

If, on the other hand, the architect is trying to win the contract to design a specific building, the model shown to the prospective client will be much more detailed. It will generally be larger, with scaled representations of as many of the features of the building as possible. Likely the roof of the model will be removable to show what the interior will look like. The architect understands that if the contract is to be won, the clearest possible picture of the proposed building must be presented to the client.

When a vision statement fails to paint a clear picture of the future, it is doomed to be relegated to the bottom drawer of a forgotten filing cabinet.

A number of yeas ago, churches scrambled to create vision statements in response to the challenge brought by the church-growth movement. Unfortunately they did so without understanding the process or the product. The result was that most vision statements were no more than elaborate mission statements and had little connection to context or reality.

When an architect designs a building he or she needs to know what the building is going to be used for and the topography of the land on which the structure will be built. Along the way, environmental studies will be undertaken to ensure that the design is in harmony with the surroundings.

I wonder how many churches when drafting their vision

statements even stop to consider their environment. Does the picture painted by the statement take into consideration their present context or one of a bygone era? Is it a picture of what might be or a collection of ideas rooted in what should be?

Failure to take environmental and contextual realities into consideration when crafting a vision statement in the end will produce a picture of the future that is unachievable. Thus, the vision that was intended to motivate becomes the source of discouragement and ultimately is banished to the "We tried that but it didn't work" file.

A pastor I have been coaching for the past couple of years was expressing his frustration over the apparent lack of desire on the part of the congregation to reach out into their community. I asked him if they had a vision statement. He responded very enthusiastically, "Absolutely," as if to say, "Of course, what church today doesn't?"

So I asked him to show it to me.

> Failure to take environmental and contextual realities into consideration when crafting a vision statement in the end will produce a picture of the future that is unachievable.

"Show it to you," he said incredulously, "I've got it memorized." The he rattled off their vision statement: "To be present and active for Jesus Christ in our community."

I knew the church and some of its history because it was part of the denomination I served in at the time. I was also familiar with the neighbourhood in which the church was located, one that had gone through quite considerable cultural change in the last 20 years. During that time many of the founding families had moved away from the community. Not all those who moved away, however, changed churches. As is often the case in this kind of urban shift, a number of the families continued to drive from the suburbs back into the city to attend the church. These families were key supporters and provided much of the financial and human resources that kept the church functioning.

I think you can see where I'm going with this. For them, being present and active had to, by necessity, mean something different than it would for someone attending the church from the community. Their approach tended to focus on traditional programming, most of which took place in the church and at times convenient to them. Meanwhile those who lived in the community saw the fulfillment of the vision from the perspective of meeting community needs. They wanted the church to be part of the community by being available to the community when they needed it. The vision, instead of uniting the congregation, was dividing them.

> The vision, instead of uniting the congregation, was dividing them.

I suggested to my friend that he needed to spend some time with his leadership team hammering out what "being present" might look like, and not just from the perspective of those who drove in. If they really wanted to craft a vision that would excite and unite the congregation, they had to listen to those who lived in the community.

If my friend was truly serious about fulfilling this vision, he would have to provide a lot more detail to elicit the congregation's support. "Being present and active" is not a picture of the future. It's a vague idea. A picture has detail and colour. It allows us to see something we might not otherwise experience. Similarly, a vision statement needs to have enough detail to provide those in ministry with a clear picture of what by God's grace might be. In other words, if you really want to excite them, you've got to show them the model with the roof off.

•••••••••••••••

"Show them the building," John thought, "that's what I have to do! But where to start?"

3

Show Them the Model

"Then Moses climbed Mount Nebo.... There the LORD
showed him the whole land—from Gilead to Dan."

Deut. 34:1

John's first inclination was to put together a team, but then
he remembered the elders' struggle to create a mission statement. Maybe it would be better if he crafted the basic outline of
the vision and then invited the elders to help shape it. This
would give them something concrete to start with and hopefully get them past the concept stage.

John was making his way from the sanctuary back to his
office as these thoughts rushed through his mind. He was a man
with a mission now and the mere thought of crafting a vision for
the church excited him.

As he dropped into his chair, his eyes scanned the bookshelf
behind his desk. He remembered seeing it the week before, one
of those books you buy at a conference and stick on your shelf

to read when you have a little spare time. In other words, never. "Well, that is about to change," he muttered aloud as he reached for the book.

The process turned out to be a little more challenging than John anticipated. The book on vision casting he had purchased at the conference wasn't as helpful as he hoped and after reading several others he found himself more confused than ever. Each of the authors seemed to have a different definition of vision and consequently a different approach to drafting a vision statement. After several attempts at drafting his own vision statement, John realized he was going to need some help. That's when he remembered his friend, Gregg, over at Union Street Baptist. They had been on the verge of closing the doors when Gregg arrived. John recalled one of the first things Gregg did was to help them discover a new vision for the church. Maybe Gregg could help him, or at the very least point him in the right direction.

Over the next few months, John worked with Gregg, using him as a sounding board for his ideas. He discovered that developing a new vision for Woodridge Community Church was much more complicated than simply scratching out a few words on a piece of paper. It required time to understand the community and its people. He was surprised at how little he knew about his neighbours, what they liked and disliked, what they did for entertainment, what they did for a living.

In the end, the process took a lot longer than John had anticipated and what started out as a crash course in vision setting ended up being a six-month journey of learning.

By the end of the second month he felt he had enough to take to the elders and a few other key leaders, so he set up a series of meetings and invited the various participants to interact with what he had prepared. Unfortunately he wasn't prepared for their response to his presentation.

Ted Fraser was the first to speak up. "What do we need a vision statement for? We have a mission statement, that's enough."

"Besides," said Mary half jokingly, "there isn't room on the golf shirts for another slogan."

It took John a while to convince them they even needed a vision statement. It wasn't until he shared with them the illustration of the building model and the roof that came off to reveal the rooms inside that they agreed to the idea.

Once they got over this obstacle, however, they jumped in with both feet, something John was not quite prepared for. Instead of simply adopting what he presented they began to take it apart.

John found himself on the defensive, justifying his ideas. He didn't like how he was responding. After all, he wanted them to own this process, but at the same time these were his ideas; he had laboured over them for over two months and in what seemed like seconds they had dismantled his work.

In the weeks that followed that fateful first meeting, John came to realize that what he understood as criticism, even downright rejection of his ideas, was in fact the process of adoption.

Because the others hadn't been part of the formation of the

vision, they had to take it apart and put it back together again before they could own it. At one point, John even wondered if he should have involved the leaders right from the beginning in the formation process. By the end he realized if he had not done the work up front they would still be haggling over the wording. "Besides," thought John, "it is my job to give direction to the church and vision is certainly a major part of its direction."

•••••••••••••••

John's struggle to know when to get the leaders involved in the process of creating a vision is not uncommon. Because "buy-in" is key to the successful execution of any plan, there is a temptation to involve multiple leaders too early in the visioning process. The result is often the "too many cooks in the kitchen" syndrome and leads to confusion, not commitment. It also runs contrary to the principle that vision begins with one person.

> John was right to believe that it was his job to give direction to the church.

John was right to believe that it was his job to give direction to the church. Indeed, that's what a vision does; it gives direction. Pastors who try to bring about vision by consensus will find there is generally more confusion than vision.

I recognize that not all pastors see themselves as visionaries. For those of you who would put yourselves in this boat, there are resources out there to help you. I highly recommend Aubrey Malphurs' book *Advanced Strategic Planning*. In the appendix, he provides the reader with a number of examples of actual vision statements. Don't be afraid to borrow the ideas. Use them to help you frame your dream. Remember, you don't have to reinvent the wheel.

And finally, don't be afraid to ask for help. Perhaps there is someone in the congregation or on your staff who is more inclined this way. If you are not comfortable looking inside the church for help, connect with another pastor in the community or in your denomination, someone you know who's been through the process and could give you some direction.

> You may not see yourself as a visionary, but we all have dreams about what we would love to see God do in our church or organization.

You may not see yourself as a visionary, but we all have dreams about what we would love to see God do in our church or organization. These dreams are the stuff vision is made of.

•••••••••••••

Once they had worked through the adoption process, John was pleased to see how excited the elders got. Tony, who had been relatively quiet during most of the sessions, suddenly spoke up. "This has been the most helpful and inspiring exercise I think I've ever participated in at this church. For the first time since we built this facility I feel like I know where we are going."

A holy silence seemed to hang over the room and in that moment they knew they were doing kingdom work.

Without any prompting, Paul, the board chair, led the group in a prayer and John was sure he saw one or two of the others dab their eyes.

As they closed the meeting, Henry, a marketing executive, leaned over to John and said, "Great job, Pastor. Let me take this to someone in our promotional department and have him put together a brochure so we can present it to the congregation."

John could barely contain himself as he drove home that night. "Thank You, Lord, for giving us a vision to serve You."

A few days later, John was in his office when he heard a knock on the door. "Sorry to disturb you, Pastor, but I thought you'd want to see these as soon as they came from the printer." It was Henry, and he was carrying a box of printed material. He walked across the office and plopped it on John's desk.

"I think you will be pleased with the job the boys in the promotional department did." He handed John a copy of the brochure. Across the top was the mission statement they had hammer out so many months ago: "Making Fully Devoted Followers of Jesus Christ." Under this was the professionally laid out statement they had laboured over for the last six months.

WOODRIDGE COMMUNITY CHURCH
VISION STATEMENT

Vision at Woodridge Community Church is about what we see God doing in us and through us as we seek to fulfill His mission in the community of Woodridge and the world. To this end:

- We envision a church where everyone is actively sharing the good news of Jesus Christ with his or her unsaved friends.

- We envision a church where everyone attending is being developed into a fully devoted follower of Jesus Christ, through contemporary seeker-friendly worship services, age-appropriate spiritual-formation classes, special events and small groups.

- We envision a church of small groups where everyone can experience authentic biblical community, where everyone is accepted and loved for who they are in Christ, and where everyone, no matter what stage they are at on their spiritual journey, can find encouragement, nurturing and forgiveness.

- We envision a church that is intentionally engaged in the equipping of its members for ministry in the church, the

> community and the world. The goal is to have every
> member of Woodridge Community Church be a minis-
> ter for Jesus Christ.
>
> • We envision a facility that serves the needs of the
>   Woodridge congregation, both in size and function, as it
>   seeks to fulfill God's mission.

This is our vision of what by the grace of God could be.

John felt like a proud new father standing at the window of a hospital nursery.

As John placed the brochure on his desk and looked up at Henry it was all he could do to keep from bursting into tears. For the first time in some years he felt the excitement that comes when we sense God is about to do a work in the life of His church.

"This is it, Henry," said John after a long silence, "the piece that was missing."

Little did John know how those words would come back to bite him.

4

WHO ARE THOSE GUYS?

"Let your light so shine before men that they may see
your good deeds and praise your Father in heaven."

Matt. 5:16

John couldn't believe what he was hearing. After all the
work they had done on the mission and vision statements how
could they reject his proposal? Didn't they understand that if
they ever hoped to see the vision fulfilled they were going to
have to change, try new things? And what was so terrible about
cancelling Sunday morning service so the church could volunteer for the hospital charity run?

The run organizers were overwhelmed when John first suggested it. They couldn't believe that a church would go to such
lengths to serve the community. He had told the chairman of
the fundraiser that he still had to run it by the board, but he was
confident that, given their new vision, they would support the
idea. Boy, was he wrong.

After a lengthy discussion, board chairman Paul spoke up. "Ladies and gentlemen, we've been at this for some time now and I have a feeling we are no closer to a decision. I appreciate where some of you are coming from. For you the church is the Sunday morning service and you feel like we would be abandoning what the church is about. This is something you hold very dear and I respect that. At the same time, John's proposal is very much in keeping with the new vision we have adopted for Woodridge Community Church, and based on the enthusiastic response given by the run organizers to Pastor John's suggestion, I think we have an obligation to be part of this important community activity. For these reasons I propose a compromise. Given that we are not needed at the run site until 9:30 a.m., why don't we hold a sunrise service for all volunteers, maybe even provide coffee and donuts after the service, before we head out to our volunteer posts? This way we can still have a service and maybe even invite some of those volunteers who don't go to a church to join us."

"Wow," thought John, "someone really does get it. This is even better than just cancelling the service. Surely they won't turn down this suggestion; after all, it is the best of both worlds."

But then Charley spoke up. "I don't know, Paul, church is supposed to be at 11 a.m.; it's always been that way. If we change it, what will people think? And what about visitors? They'll come at 11 expecting the church to have a service. What are they going to do?"

John wanted to say to him, "Charley, the whole reason we went through this visioning exercise was because we weren't seeing any visitors come; don't you get it?" But instead he kept silent and watched the discussion continue to unfold.

"I appreciate what you are saying," replied Paul. "But just because we've always done it that way doesn't make it a law. Besides, what's important here is that we worship God by serving our community, and this gives us a chance to do both. After all, Jesus did say, 'Let your light shine before men that they might see your good works and glorify your Father who is in heaven.'"

When Paul sat down you could sense that the tide had turned. Heads were nodding in agreement until finally Charley spoke up. "You know, Paul, when you put it that way I guess it really does make sense. Maybe I have been holding on to the wrong things, maybe it is time for a change."

And that's when it happened. There was no vote, no harsh exchange of words in defense of positions held, just a strong sense that God was leading Woodridge Community Church in a new direction.

After the meeting, John asked Paul to stay behind for a few minutes. He wanted to tell him how much he appreciated his leadership at the meeting and how impressed he was at the way God was working in his life.

Paul was truly touched by John's encouraging words and as he turned to leave he said, "You know, John, maybe it's time as a church we took a look at what we really value around here."

"Really value around here," thought John. "I think Paul may have something there. After all, what you value is what shapes you, and isn't that what the Sermon on the Mount is all about? Maybe it is time to take a hard look at what Woodridge Community Church values."

Even as John allowed these thoughts to pass through his mind, he realized that the journey he thought had come to an end with the formation of the vision statement was in fact far from over.

•••••••••••••

John discovered something important that night. He discovered that just like people, churches hold values and these values play an important role in shaping the culture of the church. Often they are informal and seldom written down, but they influence every decision made by leadership. They can make or break companies, organizations and especially churches.

Unfortunately, like most pastors John was unaware of the existence of these values. Consequently, when he ran into opposition or one of his ideas was not readily accepted, he attributed the lack of enthusiasm to the "we've always done it that way" syndrome. In fact what was happening was a clash of values.

For John, the value that grew out of his passion for the mission outweighed the value of the Sunday morning worship service. He concluded that cancelling the service to participate in the community activity made good sense, because "winning the lost at all cost," as the Apostle Paul put it, was the higher value.

However, he found out that night that not everyone shared his values. And for some the value wasn't just in holding a service, it was in holding a service at 11:00 a.m.

What made Paul's solution so tenable was that it acknowledged the value of holding a morning service while also upholding the value of being involved in the community for the sake of the gospel. By doing so, two competing values became co-operating values. As for the 11 a.m. service time, Paul provided a reasonable alternative in a way that allowed Charley to let go of an aspect of the value without feeling like he had let go of the whole value.

> Values play an important role in shaping the culture of the church. Often they are informal and seldom written down, but they influence every decision made by leadership.

John learned some important lessons that night about values and the key role they play in determining the direction of a church. It's all well and good to have a mission and a vision, but if you don't hold the right values you will never get to where you want to go.

Time, therefore, must be taken to identify those values that are operative in the life of a church before charting any new course. Unfortunately, because these values are seldom written down, you usually don't discover them until you run smack dab into one. It does not have to be this way, though. By asking the right questions, floating trial balloons and listening closely to what congregants say when they talk about the church, you will be able to identify many of the unwritten values that are shaping the church.

Yet it is not enough to simply identify those values. If you want to chart a new course you must be proactive in determining what values you want the church to uphold.

I remember early in my ministry we were having a problem staffing our Sunday evening children's ministry and struggling to find a time to hold our small groups. We had established small groups as an important value for the church but finding a convenient time slot in the program was becoming increasingly difficult.

At a board meeting one evening I asked the question, "Why do we have Sunday evening services?" At first the response was almost indignant, but after some discussion we came to the conclusion that the only reason we held an evening service was because we always had. In fact, we concluded that it was hin-

> By asking the right questions, floating trial balloons and listening closely to what congregants say when they talk about the church, you will be able to identify many of the unwritten values that are shaping the church.

dering us from doing a ministry we had deemed a high priority, small groups, and was even undermining our children's ministry by forcing us to provide two children's programs on Sunday, thereby burning out our workers, many of whom were doing double duty.

In a sense we had three competing values at work. One value dictated that we must have a Sunday evening service; a second had us trying to provide a children's program at that service; and the third value, one we had previously determined as a priority, was our small groups ministry. At the time we didn't call them values; we simply saw them as competing priorities. However, once we had identified these competing values it was much easier to make a decision, one in keeping with

> If you want to chart a new course you must be proactive in determining what values you want the church to uphold.

where we wanted to see the church go. It is also worth noting that when we presented our proposal to cancel the Sunday evening service and use the slot to hold our small groups we experienced very little opposition. I believe it was because we explained our decision in the context of the priorities, or values, we as the leadership had identified.

A few years after making this decision I attended a conference where I was introduced to this idea of "core values." It was as if the lights went on. The message was clear: either the leadership determines what those core values should be based on what they believe God wants to accomplish through their church, or the congregation will, by default, determine what they will be, based on personal preferences. The latter dramatically reduces the chances for the church to be all it could be for the kingdom of God.

••••••••••••••

John went home that night encouraged by the board's decision. He felt they had made a huge step toward realizing their vision.

Still, he couldn't get Paul's comment out of his mind. "Maybe its time to look at what we really value around here."

The following week John found himself revisiting the question. He asked everyone he came in contact with what they thought made Woodridge Community Church who they were. He discovered that just about everyone had a different perspective on the identity of the church. Still, there were some values that seemed to come up over and over. Family was one such value, others spoke of the role the contemporary worship played in drawing them to Woodridge and still others mentioned the importance of the missions program. Alongside of these dominant values there were a number of values that John regarded as less consequential. Someone mentioned he liked Woodridge because John still preached from behind a pulpit. Someone else mentioned how important the Ladies Missionary Group was to her, and a number of people referred to the mid-week prayer meeting.

By the end of the week John had six pages of notes, along with two dozen values that those he interviewed identified as important. "No wonder I was having a hard time getting the congregation to adopt some of my proposals," he thought. "Many of them conflict with what the congregation feels is important. This explains why Mrs. James is so opposed to small groups. She sees them as a threat to the Women's Missionary Fellowship and that's what she values most."

As John reflected over the past few years of ministry and some of the frustrations he had experienced, the pieces began to make sense. It wasn't that they disliked him or even thought his ideas were that bad; it was just a conflict of values.

"What would happen," John wondered as he sat in his study, " if instead of allowing the church's values to be determined by the congregation, the leadership was proactive in identifying those values that could shape the church in such a way as to be conducive to realizing our vision?"

"Simple enough," thought John. "I'll get the board to identify the six or seven values they believe are key to who we are as a church and help us fulfill our vision. Once established, we'll take these to the congregation, explain our reasoning and we'll be on our way."

If only it were that simple! Unfortunately, as John would soon discover, values are held more deeply than he realized. It quickly became evident that even on the board there were quite diverse opinions as to which values the church should hold and which ones should be shelved—so much so that it took several rather animated meetings before they finally settled on eight key values that represented the identity that Woodbridge Community Church desired.

THE CORE VALUES OF WOODRIDGE COMMUNITY CHURCH

Every person and organization, including the church, has a set of core values. They are the things that shape us, drive us and make us who we are. We at Woodridge Community

---

Church have decided to consciously determine what these values will be so God can shape us as He wants. They are as follows:

1. Biblical Teaching

We value the Bible as God's Word and therefore strive to teach it with integrity and authority in a way that will help seekers find Christ and believers mature in Him.

2. Authentic Worship

We value the personal and corporate worship of God in ways that embrace both creativity and authenticity.

3. Prayer

We value private and corporate prayer as part of the planning and execution of all ministries and activities of this church.

4. Grace

We value the grace of God extended to us, believing we are responsible to extend that grace to others, recognizing we are all on a journey to maturity in Christ.

5. Witness

We value lost people and believe the Bible calls all believers to be witnesses for Christ in word and deed.

6. **Community**
We value community in its corporate context and as expressed in small groups, believing everyone should be part of both.

7. **Family**
We value family and therefore are committed to its spiritual nurturing by providing an atmosphere that strengthens both marriages and families.

8. **Service**
We value serving, convinced that every believer is called to be a minister, gifted by God for meaningful service in the church and community.

As John looked over the document he wondered how it would be received. He suspected that for the most part people would endorse these values—after all, they were biblically defendable. He knew, however, he would run into difficulty when one of those values clashed with a personally held value. Hopefully his sermon series would be convincing enough that when the time came the grace value would kick in and people would be willing to let go of those personally held values for the sake of the church.

5

Getting Started

"But you will receive power when the Holy Spirit comes on you; and you will be my witnesses in Jerusalem, and in all Judea and Samaria, and to the ends of the earth."

Acts 1:8

John was sitting in his office, feet up on his desk, lost in thought. He had been reflecting on how well the sermon series on values had gone. The congregation really seemed to be getting it. There were even a few who came to him after the last message and expressed how excited they were about where the church was headed.

Unfortunately his euphoria over the values series was to be shortlived.

A loud knock on the door brought John crashing back to reality. He managed to catch his balance and breath just as he was about to topple over backwards. Grabbing the edges of his desk, he turned, and standing in the doorway was one very upset Mrs. James.

"I know what you are trying to do," she snarled. "I know where you're going with all this vision and values malarkey. You're trying to do away with my ministry. First it was the small groups getting in the way and now it's all this vision talk."

This verbal outburst caught John off guard. At first he didn't know what to say. Inside he could feel himself getting angry. He wanted to tell Mrs. James to get with the program, that she was out of touch with reality, but he managed to resist this urge and instead asked her to come in, sit down and talk about why she felt the way she did.

What transpired turned out to be one of the most helpful conversations John had had since the journey began.

The first thing John realized was that Mrs. James was a lot more in touch with what was going on than he had ever given her credit for. Because she had on a number of occasions resisted changes he was trying to make in the church he had written her off as one of those people who just didn't want to change, who opposed anything that hinted at a new idea.

As it turned out, however, Mrs. James wasn't was opposed to change; she was opposed to pointless change. She'd been around churches a lot longer than John had. She had seen pastors come and go, each one with another new idea on how they should be doing ministry, but when the idea didn't work, when the next thing didn't bring the kind of results promised, she was the one left picking up the pieces.

As John listened to Mrs. James' story, he noticed that her anger began to subside. The more she talked, the less hostile she seemed to be. Even as she wound down, John wondered how many others out there in the congregation were feeling what Mrs. James was feeling. They were nodding agreement on the outside, but on the inside they were thinking to themselves, "Here we go again."

When Mrs. James stopped speaking, John asked, "How can we make sure we don't go down the same road again?"

"I'm sorry; I'm not sure I understand what you are asking me," Mrs. James replied. "You want my opinion on how we can accomplish this vision, on how we as a church can really become what we say we value?"

"Yes," John affirmed. "After all, you are part of this church and if you are feeling the way you do about this new initiative I'm sure there are others out there who feel the same way. How do we overcome the doubters and the naysayers? How do we get them on board?"

John's question surprised Mrs. James, as she had never been asked to give her opinion at this level before.

After what seemed like an eternity, she looked at John and answered. "You know, Pastor, no one's ever asked for my input before and maybe that's the answer. Involve the people, especially those who head up the various ministries. After all aren't they are the ones who have to figure out what to do to accomplish this vision?"

It was obvious to John that he had connected with Mrs. James that day. When she left his office she was almost beside herself with excitement. What she didn't realize was that she had just given John one of the most valuable lessons he would ever learn. For people to be part of the dream, they need to be part of the process. Yes, they were starting to see the vision, but for them to own it they needed to be involved, they needed to have a hand in figuring out how they would get there.

> **For people to be part of the dream, they need to be part of the process.**

"Up until now I've been working with the elders maybe it's time to cast the net a little wider, time to involve all of the ministry leaders."

That's when it occurred to John, "I'm not sure if I know how we're going to get there. How on earth am I going to guide the ministry leaders in the process?"

●●●●●●●●●●●●●●●

John is not alone in his dilemma. Pastors are trained to teach, give counsel, care for the hearts and souls of people, not do strategic planning.

It shouldn't come as a surprise then that strategic planning is often the missing piece in ministry. It is what an executive friend of mine refers to as the "execution." He points out that churches are not the only organizations that struggle with this element. Businesses, large and small, often invest large sums of money developing mission and vision statements but fail to do the planning necessary to see the vision come to fruition.

For businesses, it's generally not a failure to plan that hampers their execution but a failure to connect the mission, vision and values to their planning. Consequently their planning is defused and therefore confused. Departments end up competing with each other because no one is sure what the desired outcome looks like. They lack a sense of cohesive direction.

Jim Collins, in his book *Good to Great*, calls this the "Hedgehog Concept."[8] Great companies are able to clearly identify the one thing they do and focus on it. Anything that does not somehow relate to that one thing holds no relevance. In other words, their mission is clear and it clearly drives their planning.

In the church, the problem is often even more fundamental than sticking to the mission. Church leaders seem reluctant to even accept the idea that the planning process is appropriate. It gets labelled as unspiritual, a tool of business that if employed by the church will result in the blatant disregard of God's plan or the leading of the Holy Spirit.

Nothing could be farther from the truth. As with any program or technique, there is always a danger of allowing it to become an end unto itself, to the

> Church leaders seem reluctant to even accept the idea that the planning process is appropriate. It gets labelled as unspiritual, a tool of business that if employed by the church will result in the blatant disregard of God's plan or the leading of the Holy Spirit.

exclusion of God's leading. But our job as church leaders is to listen to God and then, through careful planning, seek to accomplish His mission in the most effective way possible.

If the Hedgehog Concept teaches us anything it is this: for planning to be effective, it must be driven by mission, vision and values. Failure to take these into consideration when planning will result in marginal success at best and holds the potential for complete failure.

•••••••••••••••

Mrs. James was right. He had to involve more of the leadership, but involve them in what? Up until now John had been feeling his way along. The idea of mission, vision and values seemed to flow one from the other.

Then there was the vast array of leadership books. Most had something to say about these topics but often seemed contradictory to John, or at best vague about what came next. It left him feeling like he was at a dead end. They alluded to a strategic plan, but none provided any sort of description of what one might look like.

Then one day, on his way to a pastors' meeting in the next town, he grabbed a tape that had been sitting on his dashboard for some time and popped it into the player. When he heard the words of the speaker he almost lost control of his car.

"Your church can develop a strategic plan that will assist you in becoming the kind of church that God wants you to be...."[9]

John couldn't believe his ears. He listened intently as the pastor being interview talked about the role of a strategic plan, how it provides a church with a sense of focus, helps set priorities and allocate resources, and how it provides a framework for decision-making and the evaluation of new ideas.

It was as if the guy on the tape could read John's mind, answering his questions before he could even ask them.

At one point he found himself thinking, "This is all well and good if you are a church of thousands, but we are a long way from there." But before he had barely finished the thought, the speaker pointed out that strategic planning wasn't just for large churches; in fact, any church that wanted to see its vision fulfilled needed a plan.

As John listened to the speaker on the tape describe how he had pulled together the ministry leaders and how, with the mission, vision and values statements plastered on sheets of paper around the room, they worked together to develop a plan, the words of Mrs. James echoed in his mind: "Involve the people."

John now knew what he had to do.

6

THE PLAN

"'For I know the plans I have for you,' declares the LORD, 'plans to prosper you and not to harm you, plans to give you hope and a future.'"

Jer. 29:11

John watched as the various ministry leaders filed into the room. There was an obvious sense of expectation as they took their seats around the tables.

Each had received a personal invitation to an evening that had the potential to change the face of Woodridge Community Church.

By phrasing the invitation this way he hoped he would create enough curiosity to make them want to come and find out what was going on.

"Thank you all for taking the time to come out this evening; your involvement is key to the future of this church. As you are all aware, the board has been on quite a journey this past year.

"I must tell you, for all of us it has been a very steep learning curve. What started out to be a simple exercise to understand our purpose as a church has turned out to be a much more involved process than any of us could have imagined. Along the way we developed what we believe to be some very helpful and important tools for the ongoing health and growth of Woodridge Community Church.

"The tools to which I refer are of course the mission, vision and values statements we have presented to the congregation this past year. I must confess, while I had done some reading on these topics, much of it was new to me, and so we as a board were learning together.

"Each time we thought we had finished the task, someone would ask a question that would force us to dig a little deeper. I want to thank all of you, along with many others in the congregation, for not being afraid to ask the tough questions.

"It was often one of those questions or comments that spurred us on to search for the next piece of the puzzle. I'm especially grateful to Mrs. James." At this point John gave a quick glance in Mrs. James' direction and could see that she was sitting up a little taller in her chair.

"It is her insight that is really responsible for you being here this evening. She had stopped by my office to share a concern, and in the course of the conversation I asked her what she thought we should do next. I can still hear her response, 'Involve the people.'"

John turned to Mrs. James and said, "Mrs. James, you will

never know how important those words became to me. And that's why we are here, because Mrs. James suggested I invite you!"

At this, friendly laughter broke out around the room, creating a very positive, warm feeling, not to mention the heat that was being generated by Mrs. James, who by now was beaming from ear to ear.

"Like I said, much of this was new to me and so along the way I've tried to read as much as I can about leadership, the role of a board and how all that we have done fits together. I must admit this last piece really had me stymied. I thought we had finished our journey, that we had all the tools we needed to change the direction of Woodridge Community Church. Then I listened to a tape that referred to a 'strategic plan' for a church. I knew immediately this was the next piece of the puzzle we needed for Woodridge Community Church.

"There was only one problem. I had absolutely no idea how to develop a strategic plan. In fact, I'm not even sure I would know what one was if I tripped over it. And that's where Doug comes in." As he said this John gestured toward Doug, who was sitting off to the side.

"Doug and I play squash together down at the 'Y' on Tuesdays, and I was telling him about my strategic plan dilemma. It turns out Doug is a business consultant who specializes in, you guessed it, strategic planning. He told me he'd be happy to show me some basics to get me started, but then I thought, why should I try to learn how to do it and then try to teach you? Why not go right to the source? So I asked Doug if he would consider doing a little consulting with us. I even sweetened the pie by offering to let him beat me at squash. It must have worked because as you can see he's here. So without further comment, I'd like you to give a warm welcome to Doug Benson, senior planning consultant with the Target Group."

"Thanks, John," Doug began. "I'm delighted to be here. I do wish to point out, however my presence has absolutely nothing to do with you letting me win at squash. In fact, John, I'm trying to remember the last time you did beat me."

With that the room broke out in a loud burst of laughter; some even applauded. John knew he had the right guy to help him through this next phase.

"All kidding aside," continued Doug, "I'm delighted to be here, and while I must admit I've never worked with a church in this capacity before, I've come to realize non-profit organizations have to plan just like any business if they hope to grow. Now I appreciate that the growth you are looking for is a lot different than what a company might be seeking; nevertheless, it is growth, so the principles should be fundamentally the same.

"I have also come to realize over my years of working in this field we consultants have a way of complicating things so only we understand what's going on. I don't know, maybe it's a self-preservation technique." With that, laughter again filled the room and it was clear that Doug was connecting with everyone there.

"Now don't tell anyone, especially my clients, but the planning process doesn't have to be complicated and you certainly don't have to be an MBA grad to engage the process.

"I prepared a slide to help explain the process including what you have done so far, which by the way is excellent work. I only wish some of my business clients would do half the work you folks have put in."

Doug took out a pointer and began to walk the folks through the diagram he had prepared. "Those of you on the board, you started over here in this box," and he pointed to the one marked "Mission." "And rightly so, because the mission, or what some call 'purpose,' tells everyone what you do. Everything else must of necessity flow from that. You can't cast vision or determine what your values will be unless you first understand your mission. I like the way you have crystallized yours into a nice short statement. 'You need to be able to put it on a T-shirt,' is what one of my profs used to say."

With that Mary jumped up and began to parade back and forth, pointing to her T-shirt, while the rest of the room cheered her on. All this commotion caught Doug so off guard that all he could do was laugh and applaud with everyone else.

"Wow," he said when he was finally able to compose himself. "You folks have really taken this mission thing to a whole new level. Can I take you with me?" Doug asked while pointing to Mary. "I just love your enthusiasm."

When everyone was settled down in their seats again, Doug continued. "The box on the right represents your core values.

From what Pastor John tells me, you discovered that values are present and operative whether you identify them or not. You also discovered that these values can help you achieve your vision or keep you from realizing it."

By now most of the heads in the room were nodding in agreement, so Doug moved on. "This box here in the middle represents your vision; this is the picture of your preferred future. What you discovered in your journey was that mission leads to vision, and at the same time values shape vision. It would be nice if these were linear—that is, they came one after the other—but life isn't always that convenient. What happens more often than not is that these two come to bear on the visioning process simultaneously. That's why it's important to be proactive in determining not only your mission but also the values you believe are important to your organization."

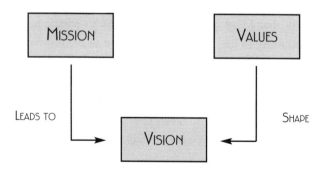

Doug stopped at this point and looked around the room. "Any questions to this point?"

There was a long silence until Fred at the table in the back spoke up. "If this stuff is so important, why don't more churches take the time to do it?"

"Good question," Doug responded. "I can't comment on why churches don't do a better job in this area, but I can tell you businesses don't do a whole lot better when it comes to visioning. I guess I should be thankful; after all, it keeps me in a job."

The room broke out in laughter again, until Karen spoke up. "I can see the value in what we have done so far, but my question is, 'So what?' I mean it's all well and good to have these nice statements, but how do we get there?"

"Great question," answered Doug. "That's why I'm here. You see, it's fine to have these statements, but unless you can turn them into some kind of plan of action they're not of much help. Which brings me to the next box, the one below the vision box."

With that Doug revealed the bottom portion of his slide. "This is the 'strategic plan,' and this strategic plan, of necessity, is driven by the vision, which means that as we plan the activities of the church they must be the kind of things that move us toward the vision."

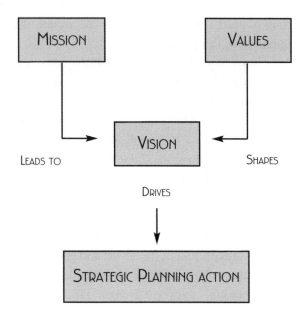

"Notice," commented Doug as he pointed to this final box, "this is the stage of the process that moves us to action."

> **All planning is designed to generate action.**

He paused for a moment and let his comment sink in and then added, "Because all planning is designed to generate action."

••••••••••••••••

John made a very strategic decision when he asked Doug to lead the team through the planning process. Some would even call it risky, given that Doug was not a believer. Yet it was strategic in that John not only understood himself and therefore his own limitations, he also understood that sometimes fresh eyes are needed. Doug had no agenda other than to help the team put a plan in place. He was free to question assumptions that those who had a stake in the organization might not otherwise question. Planning, even when driven by vision, if based on unproven assumptions runs the risk of failure.

I remember that when we first moved into our new building we had a vision to make the facility available to the community. We assumed that those who used it would become more aware of who we were and might even come out on a Sunday, or at Christmas at the very least. Given that we had the largest performance-style auditorium in the region and a full NBA-size gym, we had no end of requests. What we didn't count on were the headaches that came along with renting the facility out. There were issues surrounding staffing, security, sound and light, maintenance, not to mention policing the type of events we would permit. All of this hassle and yet, to the best of my knowledge, no significant response for the kingdom.

Now I'm not suggesting it was a mistake to rent out our building. The mistake was to make it part of our outreach strategy, based on unsubstantiated assumptions. While there were no direct program costs, and in fact it was a revenue generator, the related costs of manpower and emotional frustration gradually

> **Planning, even when driven by vision, if based on unproven assumptions runs the risk of failure.**

took away from other, more effective, ministry we wanted to do.

At the time no one questioned the assumptions. Why? Because they were mine and it was my idea, making me the ultimate stakeholder. Someone like Doug, on the other hand, would have been able to ask the right questions before the ministry idea became part of the strategic plan.

•••••••••••••••

Satisfied that everyone had processed what he had presented thus far, Doug flashed a new slide on the screen.

"Now before we actually get to the planning process, there are a few simple principles we need to review."

And with that he began walking the group through his slide.

- A Strategic Plan is a road map to the preferred future.

- A Strategic Plan must be driven by Mission and Vision.

- A Strategic Plan identifies key result areas and the corresponding objectives necessary to accomplishing the Mission and Vision.

- A Strategic Plan is of necessity both task measurable and time sensitive.

- Not everything an organization does appears on the strategic plan, rather, only those things deemed critical to the accomplishment of the mission in the allotted time frame of the plan.

When Doug finished reviewing the principles he again asked the group if they had any questions.

Charley was the first to raise his hand. "I appreciate what you are trying to do, Doug, but I just don't understand why we need to go to all this trouble. I mean, the church has been around a lot longer than most businesses, and we seem to be doing just fine."

Doug could see a few others nodding in agreement and was about to respond when Paul spoke up, "You are both right and wrong, Charley. You are correct when you suggest the church has survived down through the ages, and according to the Bible, at least as I understand, it will in the end overcome anything

Satan can throw at it. Survival is not the issue here, not if what Jesus is teaching in the parable of the 'talents' has anything to say to us. It seems to me that Jesus expects us to individually and collectively use the gifts and talents He has given us in the most effective way possible. This means, like the two faithful servants, we have to be diligent in the use of our resources, both monetary and human, and that means we need to do some planning."

John resisted an overwhelming urge to run over and hug Paul.

With that issue behind him Doug suggested they take a short break, after which he would lay out a bit of a model for them to use in their planning.

7

ONE STEP AT A TIME

The room was abuzz with conversation as the group headed towards the coffee table. It was obvious that Doug had them thinking. After about 20 minutes, John called the group back from their break. "Folks, we need to get going, the evening is fast disappearing."

Doug was already adjusting his next slide and turned just as the last of the stragglers took their seats.

"I don't know who was responsible for the coffee cake, but I'd love to add you to my seminar team along with Mary; it was delicious."

Once again the group broke into friendly laughter and John could tell Doug had won them over.

"Now you'll recall when I explain those principles I suggested that a plan is like a road map to a preferred future. Well, like any road map, there is often a map within a map. When you

> A plan is like a road map to a preferred future.

open a folded road map, the first thing you'll come across is the big picture, the map of the entire province or state. But when you begin to study the map more closely, particularly the cities, you will often find down the side a blow-up of the city that allows you to see the actual city streets and not just the major highways. In a sense this is what a strategic plan is like.

"First we will identify, using the mission, vision and values to guide us, the big-picture key-result areas. Once we have settled on these, we'll take each one individually and blow it up, or expand it in terms of detail."

Doug went to the whiteboard and drew five boxes across the top of it.

"I want you to try to think only in terms of the next two years. Now with the mission and vision in mind, what would be the three, four or even five main areas of ministry—I believe that's what you call them—you think the church needs to focus on for it to realize its vision?"

The room was quiet for what seemed like an eternity to John. It took every ounce of discipline he could muster not to jump in and prime the pump. Then the most incredible thing happened; people started to talk—not just talk, but really get into it. As fast as he could, Doug wrote the ideas in the five boxes he had drawn. John noticed that he was grouping the ideas around common themes, and when he finally called a halt to the brainstorming, all five of the boxes were crammed with words and phrases.

Doug then divided the group into five teams and assigned each team one of the boxes. "Your task," he told them, "is to decide on a single word that summarizes all of the ideas written in your box."

After about 15 minutes Doug called the teams back together again and had them share the word they had settled on to describe what was in their box. As each team reported, Doug erased what was previously in the box and replaced it with the one or two words they settled on. When he had finished writing, he stepped back and looked at the board with its five boxes now filled with only one or two words each.

OUTREACH | SPIRITUAL FORMATION | CHILDREN & YOUTH | GLOBAL MISSIONS | COMMUNITY SERVICE

"This is great," Doug commented enthusiastically as he turned back to the group. "These represent the five main areas where in the next two years you would like to see some tangible results. Is that right?"

Everyone nodded in agreement.

"Not only that, but in so doing you also believe you will be closer to realizing your vision. Does this make sense to everyone?"

Again everyone nodded agreement.

"Good." Doug continued, "Now to help us along in the planning process we need a qualifying statement under each of these words. This statement will help us develop specific objectives under each category. Let me show you what I mean.

"Take the area of 'Outreach.' What does the vision statement say you want to see happen?"

Everyone searched through their binders to find the Woodridge Community Church vision statement. Finally, as the noise of paper shuffling died out, Mrs. James spoke up. "Well, the vision statement says we want to reach the community of Woodridge with the Good News of Jesus Christ. So I guess the statement that best captures the first key result area might be simply 'To reach the community of Woodbridge with the gospel message.'"

"That's good," Doug responded, "because it tells me where you are going to primarily do your outreach, and by the way, just as importantly, it tells me where you're not going to invest your outreach efforts."

"I'm not sure I follow," interrupted Charley.

"What I mean, Charley, is that if someone comes along with an outreach idea for, say, the community of Bingham, the leadership is going to say, 'Sorry, our focus is on Woodridge, that's the area we have a vision for.'"

"But doesn't the Bible say we are to go into all the world?" countered Charley.

Paul stepped in again. "But it also says we are to be 'witnesses in Jerusalem, Judea and Samaria, and the uttermost parts of the earth,' and that sounds an awful lot like focus to me."

Charley was quiet for a moment, and then to everyone's surprise he looked over at Paul with a bit of a grin and quietly commented, "I think you've got something there, Paul. It just takes a couple of goes before it sinks into this old head of mine."

John could resist no longer. "Doug's right," he chimed in. "We can't do everything; better we do a few things well than throw a lot of mud against the wall and hope some of it sticks."

● ● ● ● ● ● ● ● ● ● ● ● ● ● ●

Doug was trying to help the leadership team at Woodbridge understand that they couldn't do everything. To be effective, they would have to learn how to focus their efforts. The planning process is a tool designed in large part to help organizations do just that, focus.

Unfortunately, because the church is called to love and accept everyone, we tend to understand this in terms of trying to be all things to all people. What we forget is that, in the same way God gifts individuals for different ministries, He gives local churches different strengths for different purposes. Just as individuals are all part of the same body, so churches are all part of the same Church and therefore share in the same mission.

When a local church body comes to terms with this, it both relieves the pressure of having to provide ministry for everyone who comes through the door and frees them up to focus on where they can be most effective for the kingdom.

● ● ● ● ● ● ● ● ● ● ● ● ● ● ●

Following the break-out time, each group presented a summary statement that defined the key result word they had been assigned. By the time the evening was over they had agreement on the five key result areas and a summary statement to describe each one.

Primary Ministry Areas

Outreach:
To reach the community of Woodridge with the gospel message.

Spiritual Formation:
To develop our congregation of Christ followers toward community, spiritual maturity and full participation within the life of the church.

Children and Youth:
To develop a children's/youth ministry that engages young people from the cradle to senior high, moving them toward spiritual maturity and service.

Global Outreach:
To develop a global outreach program that sees the church sending and supporting individuals as they respond to the call of God at home and abroad.

Community Service:
To develop a program that encourages members of Woodbridge Church to get involved in community service activities where Christ's love can be seen in action.

"Okay, folks, I think it's time we shut this session down. But before we do, I need to give your homework assignment.

"I want you to meet with your team and together come up with three or four events, or programs, or activities, whatever you want to call them, that will move you toward realizing your vision."

"There is only one rule. Whatever you put down must be measurable, both from a time perspective and in terms of numbers. For example, under outreach, if you propose an event you must say when it will be held by and how many people you hope to reach. Everyone clear?" He paused. "Good, then I will see you in three weeks." And with that he turned the evening back to John, who prayed and then dismissed them.

After everyone had left, John found Doug packing his notes into his briefcase.

"So what do you think?" asked John. "Are they getting it?"

"Absolutely," replied Doug. "I meant what I said earlier; they really are picking it up faster than many of the corporate types. No big egos to get in the way, I guess."

"I'm not so sure about that; sometimes it just takes a little longer for church folks to show their colours." John laughed. "I'm kidding, they are a great group and they really do want what's best for the church. This whole process has been a little stretching for them but very encouraging. I'm especially excited to see the way Paul has jumped in. He has become a real leader and a great friend to me."

"He sure bailed me out this evening," said Doug. "When Charley, I think that was his name, made that comment about the church surviving all these years, I knew I was in over my head."

"Yeah, Charley can do that to you sometimes, but when he's in your corner, they don't get any better."

Both men sat quietly for a moment, reflecting on the events of the evening.

Finally John broke the silence. "So what's next, Mr. Consultant?"

"Actually, John, there are two parts left to complete. First, there is what I would normally refer to as the corporate-wide objective portion of the plan. That's what I gave them to do as homework. In your case, I would call them 'church-wide ministry objectives.' Then there is the last piece of the puzzle, the piece that is often overlooked, the ministry action plans. At the end of the day, if you don't do this last step, you might as well not have bothered to do the rest. This is where the execution of the plan stands or falls."

"So what you're saying, Doug, is we still have some work to do."

"Yes," replied Doug, "but it's not as difficult as it might sound. I have some templates I use with my business clients that I think I can adapt to your circumstance. If these work the way I hope they will, it'll make the process quite manageable."

"So when do we go again?"

"I think we should give them at least two weeks to work on the project I assigned them, and then I was wondering about having an all-day session. I think we could hammer out a basic two-year plan and get started on the action planning process if we had a whole day. You don't want to drag this out any longer than you have to. You've been going at this for quite a while as it is and it's time to get some results."

John liked Doug's enthusiasm; he had a good feeling about their relationship.

•••••••••••••••

Doug had brought the group to what I believe is one of the most critical points in the process. Churches can usually identify the key result areas, but there is often a reluctance to set specific ministry targets. To do so somehow implies a lack of faith or an encroachment into God's territory. Certainly, when we do our planning and set our targets, we need to be cognizant of the need for faith. At the same time, we need to recognize what is God's responsibility and what is ours.

> Churches can usually identify the key result areas, but there is often a reluctance to set specific ministry targets.

When we set targets so low they require little or no faith to be realized, we fail to be obedient to the command "walk by faith." We are saying to God, "We are happy with things the way they are—don't ask us to move out of our comfort zone, to actually live by faith."

On the other hand, to use this as an excuse to set no goals at all or goals that even with faith are unachievable is to invite discouragement and disillusionment.

I recall our first attempt at a strategic plan. Under the primary ministry area of outreach, we initially set the target at winning 200 people to Christ over the next two years. It looked good until someone pointed out that, first of all, we don't win anyone to Christ—that's God's role. And second, given the size of the congregation and the track record of our people as it related to sharing their faith, 200 conversions seemed somewhat unrealistic.

> I can't stress enough how important it is to establish measurable targets when you are developing ministry plans. Without these you will have little chance of succeeding and the volunteers involved in the ministry will invariably get discouraged.

Instead we decided to develop programs that both taught people how to share their faith and then encouraged them to do so four times a year. Our target then became the number of people we wanted to train and the number of times we wanted them to share their faith. This then became one of the areas of prayer and ultimately encouragement as we tracked those who came to faith.

I can't stress enough how important it is to establish measurable targets when you are developing ministry plans. Without these you will have little chance of succeeding and the volunteers involved in the ministry will invariably get discouraged.

•••••••••••••

As John walked to his car that night, he felt a renewed sense of excitement for the ministry. It was as if this journey had breathed new life into both him and the leadership team of Woodridge Community Church.

"Thank You, Lord," John whispered as he slid behind the

wheel. "Thank You for the journey you have taken me on, and thank You for bringing Doug to us.... Oh, and please give me the patience to make it through the next couple of weeks."

8

THE PLAN TAKES SHAPE

"You will be my witnesses in Jerusalem, and in all Judea and Samaria, and to the ends of the earth."

Acts 1:8

John was obviously nervous as the leadership team filed in. It had been over three weeks since they last met and he wasn't sure if they had done their homework. In the intervening time one or two of the team had come to him with a question or two about their assignment, but for the most part he had let them go on their own. Doug had suggested he not get too involved with any one group but to instead give them the freedom to work on their own. This way whatever they came up with would really be theirs and they would own it.

John had to admit that letting go was a lot harder than he thought it would be. He wasn't even sure if all of the teams had met.

"Hey, John," chirped Doug as he came in the room, "good to

see you. Ready for a full day?" Then before John could answer he added, "By the way, I'm sorry I missed our squash game last week. My flight was delayed and I didn't get in until past midnight."

"No problem," quipped John. "I'm sure I would have beaten you!"

"Ya, right!" responded Doug and they both laughed.

John was about to make another comment, but before he could Doug was descended upon by Charley, who wanted to show him the work his team had done.

After being plied with coffee cake, cinnamon buns and lots of coffee, the group was ready to begin.

"Okay," shouted Doug over the din of conversations, "I want you to sit with your team at the same tables we were at the other evening.

"Now did everyone do their homework?" With that all hands went in the air. "Good," continued Doug, "that means we can get right to it. Each team has a flip chart pad on their table. I want you to write across the top of your sheet the heading you are working with and, under that, all of the ministry objectives your group came up with."

Doug watched as the teams worked on their respective lists. When it seemed like most of the teams had finished he said, "Okay, now take your sheet or sheets and stick them to the wall over there with this masking tape."

John watched as one team after another took their sheets and stuck them to the wall. It was obvious there was a sense of pride and ownership in the work each had done.

"Now," said Doug, "let's have each team explain their ministry objectives with some of the 'why' behind each."

One after another a spokesperson from each of the teams walked the group through their objectives, answering questions and providing clarity as they went.

"This is going better than I had imagined," thought John. "Maybe we will get through this without a hitch."

But then the final team got up to make their presentation. It was pretty much a given that Charley would be the spokesperson and John knew they were in for rough ride as soon as he started.

"Our primary ministry area was spiritual formation, and to be honest we had a hard time deciding what to include." Charley paused for a moment, then continued, "And so when you see our list of objectives, I think you're going to find they cross over a number of the other ministry areas."

Charley revealed a list with 15 different ministry objectives on it.

Paul was the first to jump in, "Now wait a minute, Charley. You have a project up there that involves the youth and our group was responsible for children and youth."

"I know," responded Charley, "but the youth have to develop spiritually as well, don't they? And doesn't that mean our team should include them in our planning?"

Before Paul could respond to Charley, others from the various teams began to jump into the discussion and things got pretty animated.

Just when it looked like things were getting totally out of control, Doug got up. "Okay, everyone, let's just take a step back for a moment. The struggle you are having is pretty common when it comes to the planning process. And Charley and his team are right when they say it is hard to know where to draw the lines between ministries and key result areas. But let's not forget, this is our plan, we get to draw the lines where we want, and as long as the important objectives are all taken care of, does it really matter what key result area they fall under?"

There was a long pause as the significance of what Doug said began to sink in.

"So what you are saying," questioned Charley, "when it comes to putting the plan together we have to work as a team to make sure everything we think is important gets on the plan and not worry so much about what key result area it comes under?"

"You've almost got it, Charley," answered Doug, "but you've forgotten one of the most important principles of strategic planning: not everything an organization does appears on the strategic plan, rather only those things deemed critical to accomplishing the mission in the allotted time frame of the plan. The truth is that all 15 of the objectives on your team's list are good objectives, and some of them might be better dealt with under one of the other key result areas, but given we are dealing with a two-year plan, is it realistic to think you can accomplish all of this?"

Charley was quiet for a moment, and then he responded with a smile, "What you're saying is that we have to prioritize our list and then choose the top three or four that we think we can tackle in the next two years?"

"Yes!" shouted Doug enthusiastically. "Now you're getting it!"

"But what about the other things on the list," interrupted Mrs. James, "like the Women's Missionary Fellowship?"

"Oh you don't stop doing everything else," responded Doug, "at least until you decide they are no longer moving you toward your vision. In fact, some things you will always have to do, for example, Sunday school. It's just that they won't necessarily be as strategic as other things during the time frame of the plan."

Doug could see by the expressions on their faces they were still struggling with what he was saying.

"Let me give you an example," he continued. "Let's say under the primary ministry area headed 'Children and Youth' the team decided they wanted one objective to be the hiring of a children's pastor and a youth pastor over the next two years. Now, filling just one of the positions in that two-year period is going to be a stretch. So what do we do? We determine the priority will be the hiring of a youth pastor and that's the objective that goes on the plan. It doesn't mean you stop doing children's ministry; it just means you will have to keep using volunteers until the next two-year plan is drawn up. By then, hopefully the youth pastor has been found and that objective is no longer part of the plan."

Doug paused for a moment, then asked, "Is this starting to make sense?"

Heads began to nod, as one by one they processed what Doug had just explained.

"Good," said Doug, "so let's use Charley's team's ministry objectives as a bit of an exercise. As a group you tell me which of these 15 objectives might be better dealt with under one of the other ministry areas."

After a few minutes of discussion, three of the objectives had been moved to other key result areas. "Now," said Doug, "do we all feel these other twelve belong under the spiritual formation key result area?"

Heads began to shake.

"Good," said Doug, "I think we are making progress. Maybe we should take a break here."

"Hang on a second," Paul said jumping up, "now that we've gone through the process of sorting out the spiritual formation objectives I think we need to go back and do the same for the other ministry areas. It's only fair that all of the ministry areas undergo the same assessment process, that way we can be sure we have all of our objectives under the most appropriate key result area."

Doug smiled as he turned to Paul. "That's exactly what we have to do, Paul, and as the board chair you are just the person to lead the team through the process."

Paul stepped up to the challenge and before long the group had worked its way through the list of objectives, making sure each was assigned to the most suitable key result area. When he finished, he turned to Doug and said, "So what do you think? Is this a plan or is this a plan?"

"It sure is!" responded Doug enthusiastically. "So I think this would be a good time to break for lunch. Something good is cooking in the kitchen and I know I won't be able to focus until I get a taste of it."

John took this to be a cue for him to jump in. "Wow that was great work," he said, "and those are some pretty exciting objectives. Thanks, Doug, and thank you, folks, for all your hard work. Let's give the Lord thanks for what we've accomplished and for the food we are about to enjoy." And with that John prayed and everyone made their way to the lunchroom.

John managed to catch up to Doug as he followed the rest of the group down the hall. "This is great, Doug; I never dreamed it would go so well. It looks like we have the makings of a great plan."

Doug was obviously excited, too. "We certainly do," he said. "But the work's not over yet."

"What do you mean, Doug? I thought we would just put these in the right boxes on your chart and we'd be done."

"You are partially right, and I agree that a major portion of the work is certainly done, but there is still some refining to do."

John looked puzzled. "Refining?" he asked. "What do you mean by refining?"

"Well," responded Doug, but then he stopped. "Let's not spoil what looks like a great lunch with shop talk. You will see what I mean when we get into the next session." And with that, Doug scooped up a plate and began filling it with lasagna.

••••••••••••••

The struggle Charley and his team had determining which objectives best fit under which key result areas is a common frustration in the strategic planning process. Once the categories are set, those working on the plan tend to draw somewhat rigid lines between key result areas. They forget it is their plan and they can decide where things go. There are no set rules. If something fits better under a different category or seems to belong to more than one key result area, the planners get to decide where to put it. It might even happen that enough similar objectives emerge to warrant a new key result area. A word of caution, however: don't be too quick to add new key result areas lest the plan become too large and unwieldy.

> Determining which objectives best fit under which key result areas is a common frustration in the strategic planning process.

●●●●●●●●●●●●●●

During lunch, the conversation was all about the plan. The team couldn't say enough good things about Doug and the way he had led them through the process, but it was Charley who really sealed it for John when he said, "You know, Pastor, maybe this vision and planning idea will really make a difference. I know it has sure helped me better understand what we are supposed to be doing."

John wanted to reach over and give Charley a great big hug, but he resisted. Instead, he just watched as the others at the table jumped in and shared similar sentiments.

As he watched the animated conversations taking place, the words of Mrs. James echoed in his head: "Involve the people."

"Truer words could not have been spoken," he mused.

9

SHARPENING THE FOCUS

"Let's go, folks; we still have a lot of ground to cover!" shouted Doug over the din of conversations.

Once everyone was settled at their respective tables, Doug turned from looking at the wall where the sheets had been hung and said, "You know, I think we have the makings of a good plan here, but it needs some refining. Remember the basic principles for strategic planning I gave you back when we started this process? One of them was that not everything the church does has to appear on the plan, only those things that are deemed key to reaching the vision."

"You have identified a number of great initiatives under each of the ministry objectives, in fact, probably more than could be accomplished in five years, never mind two. So what we have to do is narrow the list, refine it, so that in the end we have just those things we agree are the most strategic to accomplishing the plan."

John looked around the room and everyone seemed to be

on board they were all nodding in agreement. He had to admit Doug was good at his job.

Doug held up a bright pink card. "You will notice that there is one of these cards at each of your places. If you look at the card closely, you will see these are peel-and-stick dots. Because all of us have a tendency to think our ideas are the best ideas, we are going to help each other decide which of the many strategies should be on our plan.

"In order to do this, we are going examine each ministry area, one at a time, and choose the ministry ideas we think will best accomplish our vision. Now I want each of you to take two of your pink dots and place them on the sheet next to the ministry idea you think, over the next two years, would be most effective. Those ideas with the most dots will be the initiatives that will become part of the plan.

"Does everyone understand?" Doug paused and looked around the room. "Good, now go for it."

Immediately everyone was on their feet and moving toward the first sheet. When they had all returned to their seats, Doug flashed what looked like some sort of chart on the screen. Across the top it read "Church-Wide Ministry Objective."

"If you will all look up here you will see what I call a 'strategic plan template.' You will notice each of the five boxes corresponds to one of the five primary ministry areas that we identified earlier. Now we are going to take the top three ministry ideas from our brainstorming session and write them in the box under the corresponding ministry area. When we do, we need to make sure we include task- and time-measurable goals.

"Let me show you what I mean by taking the initiative with the most pink dots under the Outreach category.

"Most of you responded that one of the most significant things you could do to reach your community would be to 'teach people how to share their faith,' Let's take that statement and write it in this box, along with a number and a date by when we would like to have this accomplished."

Doug wrote "To train" in the first box, then stopped and turned to the group. "How many people would you like to train and by when?"

The room went silent.

Finally Paul spoke up, "Well, I would like to think we could train everyone, but I guess that's not realistic, so I'm going to suggest we set the target at 100; that would be about half of our adult attendance."

There were nods of agreement from others in the room. When Doug saw he had consensus, he added, "And when would you like to have this goal accomplished by?"

Again the room went silent, until Mrs. James spoke up. "I think we could have all 100 trained by the end of the second year."

This time there was more discussion. Some felt they ought to be able to accomplish the goal in less than two years; others felt it might take longer. Doug let the discussion go on for a time and then he waded in.

"It's good that we have some discussion taking place," he

said. "It's an important part of the process; it creates ownership. What we need to remember when we are working with both the targets and the time frames is that they need to be somewhat realistic but at the same time stretch us. I think Pastor John would call it faith. In other words, the targets or goals must demand a measure of faith. We also need to remember this is a two-year plan, and so at the very outset, our time targets must fit within the context of the plan time frame."

He then turned back to the boxes and wrote:

• To train 100 people to share their faith by June of 2010

"How does that sit with you?" he asked the group. Everyone nodded in agreement. "Good. Now I want each of the five groups to do what we just did together for the top three ideas on the sheets. Each group is to do this for the ministry area you worked on."

The teams quickly got down to it and when the room finally went silent they found themselves staring at what they all agreed was a pretty good plan.

"Ladies and gentlemen, I want to congratulate you. I can't say for sure but if God is watching, my guess is that He is smiling at what you are going to try to accomplish over the next two years. At the very least, it will, as you say, demand faith."

With that, Doug looked over to John and said, "This would probably be a good time to take a break, but before we do, John, do you want to comment? After all, you are the one will be overseeing the execution of the plan."

"I will," he stammered as he looked back at Doug, feeling the weight of Doug's words.

"Oh," said Doug, "I guess I forgot to tell you about that part." This immediately brought a gale of laughter from the group.

"Thanks a lot," responded John. "I'll remember that the next time we play squash! All kidding aside, you folks have done a great job and I'm especially excited to see what you want to accomplish for God over the next two years. I really feel like we are in this together. I must admit that it does scare me a little, which is why I think it is important for us as a group to take some time here today to pray for God's wisdom as we move forward."

John led in prayer and others joined in. After most in the room had prayed, he closed the prayer time, and there was a simultaneous "Amen."

As folks were headed toward the coffee machine, Doug spoke up. "We're almost there, folks, just one more piece. When we come back from break I'm going to show you how to turn the plan into action."

●●●●●●●●●●●●●●

When it comes to setting targets, most churches, and for that matter most individuals, struggle with the idea. We resist because we know that once we establish a measurable goal we are forced to deal with the possibility of failure, and no one likes to fail. Unfortunately, this resistance to setting goals in context of the church can often be justified under the guise that it is somehow unspiritual. It's not about numbers or targets, opponents will argue. God is more concerned about people.

This argument sounds good until you read in Acts 2:41, "about three thousand were added to their number that

> We resist because we know that once we establish a measurable goal we are forced to deal with the possibility of failure, and no one likes to fail.

day." Somebody had to have counted, but not only that; God thought it important enough to have Luke record it.

I think there is, however, more to establishing goals than just the numbers issue. It is in our nature to resist being held accountable. From Adam and Eve on down, it is the issue that has kept us from God.

Consequently, when it comes to planning and we are asked to quantify our goals, we resist because we know that when we do, someone will hold us accountable.

What we fail to understand when we refuse to set goals is that we have no way of evaluating our effectiveness. The Apostle Paul

> What we fail to understand when we refuse to set goals is that we have no way of evaluating our effectiveness.

instructed the Ephesians to make "the most of every opportunity" (Eph. 5:16). To do this, however, requires that we know if our efforts are in fact effective. How will we know, for example, if we have gone into all the world, as the Great Commission commands, if someone doesn't keep track of where the gospel has and hasn't been preached? This is a measurable goal.

A strategic plan with measurable objectives, driven by godly values and a biblical mission, is not about success or failure as much as it is about increasing our kingdom effectiveness.

10

A TIME FOR ACTION

"Therefore go and makes disciples of all nations, baptizing in the name of the Father and of the Son and of the Holy Spirit, and teaching them to obey everything I have commanded you."

Matt. 28:19-20

John had to admit he was a little nervous as the team moved back to their places. Up to this point he was pretty much in step with where Doug had taken them and the way he had walked them through the process had made good sense. But this final step—putting the plan into action—this was the part he wasn't sure about. He had tried this action planning before, but it always seemed so complicated, especially when it came to working with volunteers. John was curious about how Doug would get buy-in from the leaders.

"Okay, folks," shouted Doug, "let's get started. This final step is without a doubt the most critical piece in all we have done so far." Doug wrote the word "execute" on the white-board.

"Ultimately, if we don't execute, all of the other things we've done have been a waste of time."

It was obvious from the expressions of those in the room that he had everyone's attention.

"It is at this point most organizations drop the ball." He paused for effect. "And the reason I think they do is because of the 'A' word… that's right, the 'A' word: *accountability*. We like to talk about it, but when it comes right down to it, most people are afraid of it. Afraid, because we think it will set us up to fail. On the contrary, when we are held accountable for something, it usually means we are more likely to succeed.

"To help with the process I'm going to show you how to use a tool that will not only facilitate the accountability, it actually empowers people. It will empower them because it clearly defines what is expected of them, and when people know what is expected of them, they are much more likely to perform more effectively."

Paul spoke up. "You know, that makes good sense, Doug. When my team at work knows exactly what's expected of them, they do a much better job and in fact there is a much stronger sense of team."

"That makes sense," Fred jumped in, "when there is a pay-cheque involved, but we are primarily a volunteer organization. How well do you think it will work here?"

"Well, that's what we are about to find out," replied Doug. "One thing I do know, even with my very limited understanding of the Bible, is that accountability seems to be pretty high on God's agenda."

There were nods of agreement from just about everyone in the room on that one.

"Okay, with that in mind, we want to do two things in the time that remains. First I want to show you an 'action planning' technique, then we will assign responsibility for each of the objectives on our strategic plan."

Doug moved to his laptop and pressed one of the keys. Immediately an image appeared on the screen at the front.

ACTION PLAN TITLE:

ACTION PLAN SUMMARY DESCRIPTION:

ACTION PLAN STEPS:

Doug explained, "In this top box we are going take one of the ministry-wide objectives from our strategic plan and shorten it down to a couple of words. So, for example, the objective of training people to share their faith might be shortened to what?"

"How about 'evangelism training,'" suggested Mrs. James.

"Sounds good," Doug wrote "evangelism training" in the title box. "Now for the action plan summary box—anyone want to take a shot at this?"

The room went quiet for a moment.

Mark, one of the small group leaders, spoke up. "How about, 'To train 100 people to share their faith'?"

"That works, except for one thing," responded Doug. "We can't forget the qualifier 'by June 2008.'" And he wrote that down.

"Now for the action steps—the specific things we need to do to realize this objective by the given date.

"I suggest when you are doing this part you take another piece of paper and list all of steps you need to take to accomplish this goal. Don't worry too much about the order for the moment; let's just break it down into its various components."

Doug moved to the whiteboard and began to list the steps as they were shouted out to him.

"Form a training team."

"Good," responded Doug enthusiastically, "but how many do you want on the team and when do you want it formed by?"

"I think three people would do it," said Paul.

"And if we want to get this done by June 2008," inserted Jan, "we need to get going. So I'd say the team needs to be in place by this June—that way they can have the training program up and running by the fall."

Doug wrote "form a training team of three by June 2008."

Doug continued to challenge them to provide specific numbers and dates until they had listed all the necessary steps. Once the list was complete, he wrote them in the action plan step box, putting them in chronological order as he went.

"And that's a wrap," said Doug as he finished writing the

last step on the board, turned and threw the whiteboard pen in the air like the weather guy on TV. "I do believe we've got our first action plan."

Everyone in the room applauded and you could tell they were catching the excitement.

When they had quieted down, Doug started in again. "Okay folks, this is just the first one. Now we have to do the same thing for each of the ministry objects on the plan."

There was a collective groan in response to Doug's comment.

"I know, I know, you thought you were finished, and in fact as a group we are almost finished. Rather than have all of you as a group come up with plans for each of the objectives, we are going to assign the various objectives to individuals to develop the action plans. This is the ownership part I referred to earlier."

Doug moved over to the walls where the flip chart sheets of the ministry-wide objects had been taped up.

Pointing to the first sheet, Doug said, "We need to put a name beside each of these objectives. This will be the person who owns it and who will be responsible to develop the action plan."

"Now before you panic, know that I won't abandon you. Once you've written out your plan for the objective you are responsible for, I want you to e-mail it to me. I'll go over it and make any suggestions I think might be helpful. When we have all the plans in their final form, I'll have my assistant put them in a common format and give a copy to everyone."

Most of the folks in the room looked relieved to know Doug was going to help them.

Mark spoke up again. "You know, Doug, when we started this whole strategic planning process I was pretty skeptical. After all, what does someone from the business world know about church? We're not a business. And then when you told us today that this action planning process would really empower people, I really had my doubts. If anything, I thought it would scare people away. But now, having worked our way through it I have to tell you I'm convinced we are on the right track. I just want to thank you and ask you to forgive me for thinking that someone like yourself who's not part of this church couldn't teach us something."

Doug was so taken aback by Mark's comments that he just sat there in silence. A moment later applause broke out along with shouts of "Thanks, Doug" and "Great job, Doug."

When things quieted down, Doug turned to John and said, "Well, I think this is where I turn it over to you." With that, Doug tossed him the whiteboard pen.

"But we haven't assigned ownership yet," protested John as he grabbed at the air for the pen.

"I know," said Doug, "but I think you know these folks better than I do, so assigning responsibility is probably something you're better equipped to do."

"Well, okay," responded John, pointing to the first objective on the sheet, "who wants to own this one?"

A hand went up and John wrote the name beside the objective. He repeated the process, working his way down the sheets until he came to the last one.

"Alright," said John, "we're down to the last objective; who's willing to take this on?"

The room went silent and no one raised a hand. John waited for a moment, then he read the ministry objective out loud. "To participate in four community-driven activities by June 2008." He waited to see if someone would bite. Still no takers. Finally he said, "Surely someone is up to the challenge?"

Again there was a long silence, until one lone voice emerged. It was Mrs. James.

"I guess I can give it a try," she said reluctantly. Everyone applauded.

Then she added, "But I haven't got a clue where to start."

At this point John wasn't sure what to do. He didn't want to make someone responsible for an objective who really didn't have a heart for it, but what could he do? He turned to Doug as if to say, "Help me out here, buddy."

Doug picked up on John's desperation and moved to the whiteboard. "Mrs. James, why don't we use your ministry objective as a final example of how to do an action plan? We'll do it together, just to make sure everyone understands the process."

"That works for me," said John as he handed Doug the marker.

"I'm for that, too," replied a relieved Mrs. James.

"So what will the action plan title be?" asked Doug.

Mrs. James thought for a moment, then replied, "How about 'Community Involvement Projects'?"

"I think that will work," said Doug, and he wrote it at the top of the board.

"Now how about the action plan description?"

"To have the church members participate in four community-driven activities by June 2010."

"That should also work," responded Doug as he wrote it below the title.

"Now, Mrs. James, what is the first thing you think you need to do?" asked Doug.

Mrs. James hesitated for a moment. "Well, I guess I need a team to work with me."

"Good, let's write that down. How many people do you think you'll need on your team?"

"Well," said Mrs. James, "there are four events, so I think four would be a good number."

Doug wrote, "Identify four individuals for team by...." Doug waited with the pen poised to write in a date.

"By June 30, 2010," said Mrs. James.

"And the next thing you need to do?" Doug asked.

Without missing a beat, Mrs. James shouted out, "Call a team meeting by September 1, 2010."

"Good," encouraged Doug, "you're getting the hang of this! What's next?" he asked, looking back over his shoulder in her direction.

"I guess I need to help them make an action plan for the team?" she wondered aloud.

"You are a fast learner, Mrs. James, that's exactly right. I was afraid you were going to start to try to plan what the team would do, but I think you realized that is for them to do."

It was obvious Mrs. James was feeling pretty good about herself. "You know, Pastor John," she said," I wasn't sure I could do this, but now that we've broken it down and I see I don't have to do all the work, I really think I *can* do it!"

Once again the group cheered for Mrs. James and John realized action planning wasn't just a tool to get things done, it was a way to empower people.

●●●●●●●●●●●●●●

Like many pastors and leaders of volunteer organizations, John assumed that people don't like to volunteer. They are too busy and they certainly don't want to be held accountable. In fact, nothing could be farther from the truth. More than ever, people are looking for significance and fulfillment through volunteer work. However, before they get involved they want to know what exactly is expected of them and how much time it will take.

Providing them with this information through an action plan helps volunteers decide not only if they can commit to the task but also whether they feel they are equipped to carry it out.

Often a volunteer will be reluctant to take on a ministry because the task seems overwhelming. An action plan breaks down a task into doable pieces, making it possible for even the most reluctant volunteer to succeed. When we help volunteers succeed, we empower them. This tends to have a ripple effect. When people succeed at a task, they feel good about it. This good feeling translates into confidence,

> More than ever, people are looking for significance and fulfillment through volunteer work. However, before they get involved they want to know what exactly is expected of them and how much time it will take.

which opens the door to further involvement, often of a more challenging nature, and that is empowerment.

There are a couple of added benefits to the action planning process. With staff, the action plans provide an objective basis for job performance evaluations. As a senior pastor I was often frustrated with members of my staff because they were not performing up to my expectations. I didn't know they were equally frustrated, first, because I didn't always communicate my expectations clearly, and second, because I failed to set reasonable completion time frames.

The action planning process provided a tool that allowed us to determine what exactly had to be done and the time frame in which it was to be done. In this way, the staff member who put together an action plan for a ministry or task was setting the expectation by which he or she wanted to be evaluated. This went a long way towards reducing frustrations and helped us work together much better as a team.

With volunteers, the action plan becomes a tool, helping the leader serve more effectively. As a pastor, I often found myself taking back a ministry that I had handed off to someone because the job wasn't getting done. Thinking I was helping the volunteers by stepping in, I was in fact hurting them. My action communicated that I didn't think they were capable. The action planning process provided me with the information I needed to serve that leader without taking over and undermining the volunteer. If a leader was stuck on any given step of the plan, I could offer to help in that one area and then step back until I was needed again. In this way the action plans become tools of empowerment and encouragement in the hands of a pastor.

> With volunteers, the action plan becomes a tool, helping the leader serve more effectively.

●●●●●●●●●●●●●●

The day ended with everyone feeling excited about their respective parts and the ministry objectives they were responsible for. Finally they had been given a tool they could really use and they were excited to see what God was going to do through them.

Paul rose from his seat. "I think we all have to agree," he began, "that today has been, for our leadership team, one of the most helpful times we have ever shared." He paused and looked around the room before continuing. "And there are two people we need to thank."

"First, I want to say thank you to Pastor John for having the courage to take us on this journey. John, I know these past months have been a challenge; who could have known it would take us over 18 months to get where we are today? Let me just say, on behalf of the leadership, that it was worth it and I thank God for your leadership."

"I also need to say a word of thanks to Doug, who stepped outside of his comfort zone to come and share these principles with us. I'm not sure if you realize it, Doug, but God has used you to further His kingdom. Thanks from the bottom of our hearts. I hope we will see more of you."

Once again the group broke into applause and cheers. When they finally quieted down, Paul said, "Let's close our session by praying together."

They all stood and formed a circle, including Doug, and Paul prayed.

EPILOGUE

John again found himself sitting at the back of the auditorium, but things looked a lot different than that first time when he wondered what it would take to get the folks to move closer to the front, closer to the action. A lot had happened and truly he was not the same person.

After the action planning process was complete, the elders presented the whole package to the congregation. There were a few questions, but for the most part the congregation embraced it. After all, many of them had a hand in putting it together. "Involve the people." John could still hear Mrs. James' words.

Of course it wasn't all roses—it never is in the real world—and even the best plans can get off track. Leaders changed; some of the objectives were unrealistic and had to be reassessed. But overall the church was making progress and they were seeing real growth, both in the numbers and in the lives of individuals.

Paul emerged as an outstanding leader and was an indispensable help to John. The action plans themselves became part of John's ministry toolbox. He found himself constantly reviewing them to see where he might serve a leader or a ministry. More than once, he surprised a leader by asking how a meeting went or if the workers needed to do a ministry had been recruited. On one occasion he showed up at the Community Involvement Team's meeting and asked what he could do to help. It turned out they need a contact at city hall and John was able to give them a name. Mrs. James was thrilled.

"We certainly have come a long way in these past two years," he thought to himself.

And that's when it hit him, the realization they were almost at the end of the two-year plan and it was time to start the process all over.

"But this time will be different," he said out loud as he stood to his feet. "This time we know where we are going."

•••••••••••••

You have probably guessed there is no Woodridge Community Church and Pastor John's story is fictional. Yet I am convinced that this story is typical of many pastors in North America today. In part it is my story.

I was blessed to be pastor of a growing church, but it was not without its struggles. John's journey to discover the role of mission, vision and values is in many ways my journey. For many years, I "threw a lot of mud against the wall," as John so eloquently put it. Fortunately, some of it stuck, yet all the while I felt in my gut there had to be a better way to do things.

I am particularly grateful to God for sending me individuals who were willing to step outside their comfort zones to share their skills and giftedness to help me understand many of the principles I've tried to share in this book. The final piece, action planning, came at a time in my ministry when I was probably the most frustrated with my leadership skills, to the point where I was wondering if I should continue being the team leader. Thanks to the process of action planning, we were able to turn things around, making the last couple of years some of the most productive and enjoyable of my ministry.

Believing God was calling me to share my experiences with other pastors and leaders, I left the church that had been my life and steady source of income for 21 years to walk by faith. As always, God has proven faithful and through the generous support of friends, has allowed me to continue serving him as the executive director of the Tyndale University College & Seminary Centre for Leadership, Toronto, Canada, and as a church consultant and coach with Life Change Consulting. It is in my capacity as a church consultant that I have come to appreciate how valuable and important this material is for the local pastor, regardless of church size.

Like it or not, pastors are called to be not only teachers and caregivers, but also leaders and administrators. It is my sincere hope that the tools I have shared will be of help to you in your capacity as a leader as we journey together, serving the living God and His church.

APPENDIX

The following pages are designed to help you apply the planning process outlined in Pastor John's story. As was mentioned in the introduction, you are free to use them in your own planning. It is important to remember as you begin this process that it has to be constantly reviewed and modified in response to changing environmental circumstances. Churches that fail to recognize the ongoing changes in their community will find themselves planning for people who aren't there. I recommend a two-year cycle. Those projects requiring longer cycles, such as buildings, can be carried over from one plan to the next along with any projects that upon review continue to move you toward your vision. With this in mind, may God use these principles to help you serve Him more effectively.

Mission is what you do, and for churches that means the Great Commission. Thus, all churches have essentially the same mission. It can be both contemporized and contextualized, i.e., by using the name of your church in the statement, but at the end of the day it had better reflect the Great Commission. As you prepare your mission statement, remember the following principles.

Take some time to write out the mission statement of your church. Remember, this is not a vision statement, but rather a statement that identifies what we do as a church. It is the answer to the question, "Why does the church, your church, exist?"

MISSION
- Mission is what you do.
- A mission statement articulates what you do in a single sentence.
- The essence of a mission statement should be reducible to one or two words.

Vision is where you are going. It is a detailed description of the future you believe if realized will position the church to most effectively carry out the mission.

Take some time to write out the vision statement for your church. Is it detailed enough to paint a clear picture of what could be?

Hint: When writing a vision statement, begin by writing it in paragraph form, rather than a series of statements, as if you were writing a letter to someone describing a scene. This will force you to include details you might otherwise omit. You can then go back and edit your description of the preferred future into appropriate statements.

VISION
- Vision is where you are going.
- Vision is a picture of the preferred future.
- A vision statement is therefore a series of sentences that paint a clear picture of that preferred future.
- A vision statement should inspire people to join with you in accomplishing the mission.

Core values are what defines who you are. These values are present in every organization and are most often not written down. Identifying these values and determining which ones are helpful along with what values are missing is critical to realizing the vision.

CORE VALUES
• Values are who you are.
• Values are beliefs held by those who make up an organization.
• Values shape the culture of an organization.
• Because values are deeply held beliefs, they have the power to hinder or advance the mission.
• Organizations therefore need to be proactive in identifying and instilling those values that will be most conducive to accomplishing its mission.

1. **What values does your congregation presently hold?**
Have each member of the leadership team interview a number of individuals, asking them what they value about your church. Record the responses and identify those that come up most often.

2. **What values does the congregation need to hold in order to accomplish the vision and mission of the church?**
With the mission and vision statements in hand, list the nine or

ten values you as a leadership team need to hold in order to realize your mission and vision.

3. Now compare the two lists, identifying those areas where the congregation already holds the appropriate value and those areas where there is a clash in values. These are the areas that will have to be worked through to ensure everyone is going in the same direction.

The strategic plan is your road map to the preferred future. It is, by God's grace, how you will proceed toward realizing the vision you believe God has given you.

Strategic Plan
- A strategic plan is a road map to the preferred future.
- A strategic plan must be driven by mission and vision.
- A strategic plan is by default shaped by values.
- A strategic plan identifies key result areas and the corresponding objectives necessary to accomplishing the mission and vision.
- A strategic plan is of necessity both task measurable and time sensitive.
- Not everything an organization does appears on the strategic plan, rather only those things deemed critical to the accomplishment of the mission in the allotted time frame of the plan.

---

1. Using your mission, vision and value statements and the template provided, identify the four or five key result areas you would like to focus on for the next two years.

2. Give a one- or two-word heading to each of these areas and insert it into the boxes at the top of the chart. These are the "Primary Ministry Areas."

3. In the same box write a write a statement that delineates what you want to do in a broad way in that primary ministry area (see example).

4. Now in the corresponding boxes under "Church-Wide Ministry Goals" enter the specific goals you are going to work toward in those categories. Remember, they must be measurable.

5. Repeat the process for each of the primary ministry areas.

6. Now assign responsibility for each of the goals, writing in the name of the person or group who will be held accountable for carrying out that goal.

Ministry Plans

Primary Ministry Objectives

Outreach:
To reach the GTA East with the gospel message.

Spiritual Formation:
To develop our congregation of Christ followers toward community, spiritual maturity and full participation within the life of the church.

Global Missions:
To partner with mission organizations to bring God-directed transformation throughout the world.

Community Service:
To mobilize our congregation to demonstrate Christ's compassion for the broken in our community.

Relational Evangelism:
- To have 400 people share the gospel with one other person by June 2006.
- To have 50 baptisms by June 2006.

Worship Services:
- To achieve an average attendance of 1,200 in worship services by June 2006.

Small Groups:
- To establish a total of 105 small groups by June 2006.

Leadership Training:
- To have 60 team leaders attend one training session by June 2006.

Community Projects:
- To involve 100 people in specific community projects by June 2006.
- To establish 5 ministry team leaders with a heart and passion for community service projects by June 2006.

Short-Term Missions Projects:
- To have 20 people participate in short-term mission projects by June 2006.

Missions Awareness:
- To educate 200 people in global missions by June 2006.

127

The action plans are the final pieces in the puzzle. Now that you have your road map to the preferred future, the "Strategic Plan," it's time to start down the road to your destination. The action plans are what get you to where you want to go. As you develop them remember the principles (see sample page 129):

Action Plan

• Action plans convert conceptual objectives into measurable actions.

• Action plans are the detailed steps required to accomplish a specific objective.

• Action plans are developed in response to a specific objective and are therefore tied to a key result area of the plan.

• The specific steps of an action plan are time sensitive and/or measurable.

Action Plan Title:
Relationship Evangelism

Action Plan Summary Description:
To have 400 people share their faith with one other person by June 2008.

Action Plan Steps:
• Identify 5 people to be on organizing team by Oct. 2010.
• Call organizing team meeting by Nov. 1, 2010.
• Have team select training program by Dec. 15, 2010.
• Hold first training session by Jan. 30, 2011.
• Develop reporting system to follow up those who share their faith by Feb. 20, 2011.
• Create forum for those who share their faith to tell their story by March 1, 2011.
• Hold second training session by June 1, 2011.
• Hold third training session by Nov. 30, 2011.
• Continue holding training sessions as required.*

* Various members on the team will be assigned tasks from the action plan. They will in turn develop action plans for their assigned tasks and be accountable to the team.

ENDNOTES

1 Aubrey Malphurs, *Leading Leaders: Empowering Church Boards for Ministry Excellence* (Grand Rapids: Baker Book House, 2005), 14.

2 Ibid., 14.

3 Reginald Bibby, *Restless Churches: How Canada's Churches can Contribute to the Emerging Religious Renaissance* (Ottawa: Novalis, 2004).

4 Rick Warren, *The Purpose Driven Church* (Grand Rapids: Zondervan Books, 1995), 98.

5 Aubrey Malphurs, *Advanced Strategic Planning: A New Model for Church and Ministry Leaders* (Grand Rapids: Baker Book House, 2005), 151.

6 Aubrey Malphurs, *Advanced Strategic Planning*, 134.

7 Ibid., 151.

8 Jim Collins, *Good to Great: Why Some Companies Make the Leap... and Others Don't* (New York: HarperBusiness, 2001).

CASTLE QUAY BOOKS